Nefertiti in the Flak Tower

ALSO BY CLIVE JAMES

CLIVE JAMES

Nefertiti in the Flak Tower

COLLECTED VERSE 2008–2011

PICADOR

First published 2012 by Picador
an imprint of Pan Macmillan, a division of Macmillan Publishers Limited
Pan Macmillan, 20 New Wharf Road, London N1 9RR
Basingstoke and Oxford
Associated companies throughout the world
www.panmacmillan.com

ISBN 978-1-4472-0700-9

Printed and bound by CPI Group (UK) Ltd, Croydon, CRO 4YY

To Christian Wiman

Acknowledgements

My thanks to the editors of the *New Yorker*, *Poetry (Chicago)*, the *TLS*, the *Spectator*, the *New Statesman*, *Poetry Review*, *Standpoint*, the *Australian Literary Review*, the *Australian Book Review* and *Quadrant*. Owing to an oversight on my part, "Dreams Before Sleeping" was printed in *Angels Over Elsinore* with one crucial line missing, so I have given the poem another run. "Special Needs" is in my volume of selected poems *Opal Sunset* but since I neglected to include it in *Angels Over Elsinore* it lacked a volume to be selected from, so to speak: hence its inclusion here. Otherwise all these poems are making their first appearance in volume form. Once again I am grateful to Don Paterson for his detailed comments and for choosing the order.

Contents

Signing Ceremony

Hotel Timeo, Taormina

The lilac peak of Etna dribbles pink,
Visibly seething in the politest way.
The shallow vodka cocktails that we sink
Here on the terrace at the close of day

Are spreading numb delight as they go down.
Their syrup mirrors the way lava flows:
It's just a show, it might take over town,
Sometimes the Cyclops, from his foxhole, throws

Rocks at Ulysses. But regard the lake
Of moonlight on the water, stretching east
Almost to Italy. The love we make
Tonight might be our last, but this, at least,

Is one romantic setting, am I right?
Cypresses draped in bougainvillea,
The massed petunias, the soft, warm night,
That streak of candy floss. And you, my star,

Still walking the stone alleys with the grace
Of forty years ago. Don't laugh at me
For saying dumb things. Just look at this place.
Time was more friend to us than enemy,

And soon enough this backdrop will go dark
Again. The spill of neon cream will cool,
The crater waiting years for the next spark
Of inspiration, since the only rule

Governing history is that it goes on:
There is no rhythm of events, they just
Succeed each other. Soon, we will be gone,
And that volcano, if and when it must,

Will flood the slope with lip-gloss brought to boil
For other lovers who come here to spend
One last, late, slap-up week in sun-tan oil,
Their years together winding to an end.

With any luck, they'll see what we have seen:
Not just the picture postcard, but the splash
Of fire, and know this flowering soil has been
Made rich by an inheritance of ash.

Only because it's violent to the core
The world grows gardens. Out of earth we came,
To earth we shall return. But first, one more
Of these, delicious echoes of the flame

That drives the long life all should have, yet few
Are granted as we were. It wasn't fair?
Of course it wasn't. But which of us knew,
To start with, that the other would be there,

One step away, for all the time it took
To come this far and see a mountain cry
Hot tears, as if our names, signed in the book
Of marriage, were still burning in the sky?

Monja Blanca

The wild White Nun, rarest and loveliest
Of all her kind, takes form in the green shade
Deep in the forest. Streams of filtered light
Are tapped, distilled, and lavishly expressed
As petals. Her sweet hunger is displayed
By the labellum, set for bees in flight
To land on. In her well, the viscin gleams:
Mesmeric nectar, sticky stuff of dreams.

This orchid's sexual commerce is confined
To flowers of her own class, and nothing less.
And yet for humans she sends so sublime
A sensual signal that it melts the mind.
The hunters brave a poisoned wilderness
To capture just a few blooms at a time,
And even they, least sensitive of men,
Will stand to look, and sigh, and look again,

Dying of love for what does not love them.
Transported to the world, her wiles inspire
The same frustration in rich connoisseurs
Who pay the price for nourishing the stem
To keep the bloom fresh, as if their desire
To live forever lived again through hers:
But in a day she fades, though every fold
Be duplicated in fine shades of gold.

Only where she was born, and only for
One creature, will she give up everything
Simply because she is adored; and he

Must sacrifice himself. The Minotaur,
Ugly, exhausted, has no gifts to bring
Except his grief. She opens utterly
To show how she can match his tears of pain.
He drinks her in, and she him, like the rain.

He sees her, then, at her most beautiful,
And he would say so, could she give him speech:
But he must end his life there, near his prize,
Having been chosen, half man and half bull,
To find the heaven that we never reach
Though seeking it forever. Nothing buys
Or keeps a revelation that was meant
For eyes not ours and once seen is soon spent:

For all our sakes she should be left alone,
Guarded by legends of how men went mad
Merely from tasting her, of monsters who
Died from her kiss. May this forbidden zone
Be drawn for all time. If she ever had
A hope to live, it lies in what we do
To curb the longing she arouses. Let
Her be. We are not ready for her yet,

Because we have a mind to make her ours,
And she belongs to nobody's idea
Of the divine but hers. But that we know,
Or would, if it were not among her powers
Always across the miles to bring us near
To where she thrives on shadows. By her glow
We measure darkness; by her splendour, all
That is to come, or gone beyond recall.

Stage Door Rocket Science

In the early evening, before I go on in Taunton,
I'm outside the stage door for a last gasp.
Two spires, one Norman, share the summer sky
With a pale frayed tissue wisp of cirrostratus
And the moon, chipped like the milky white glass marble
I kept separate for a whole week and then ruined
By using as a taw.

I have never been here before,
So where does this strong visual echo come from?
Concentrate. Smoke harder. And then I get it:
Cape Kennedy, the rocket park in the boondocks.
A Redstone and a Jupiter stuck up
Through clear blue air with a cloud scrap just like this one,
And the moon in the same phase.

The rockets, posing for the tourist's gaze,
Were the small-time ancestors of Saturn V,
But so were these spires. It's a longer story
Than the thirty years I just felt shrink to nothing.
Time to go in, get rigged with the lapel mike –
Its furry bobble like a soft black marble –
And feel the lectern shaking while I set
Course for the Sea of Shadows.

A Perfect Market

ou plutost les chanter

Recite your lines aloud, Ronsard advised,
Or, even better, sing them. Common speech
Held all the rhythmic measures that he prized
In poetry. He had much more to teach,
But first he taught that. Several poets paid
Him heed. The odd one even made the grade,
Building a pretty castle on the beach.

But on the whole it's useless to point out
That making the thing musical is part
Of pinning down what you are on about.
The voice leads to the craft, the craft to art:
All this is patent to the gifted few
Who know, before they can, what they must do
To make the mind a spokesman for the heart.

As for the million others, they are blessed:
This is their age. Their slap-dash in demand
From all who would take fright were thought expressed
In ways that showed a hint of being planned,
They may say anything, in any way.
Why not? Why shouldn't they? Why wouldn't they?
Nothing to study, nothing to understand.

And yet it could be that their flight from rhyme
And reason is a technically precise
Response to the confusion of a time
When nothing, said once, merits hearing twice.

It isn't that their deafness fails to match
The chaos. It's the only thing they catch.
No form, no pattern. Just the rolling dice

Of idle talk. Always a blight before,
It finds a place today, fulfills a need:
As those who cannot write increase the store
Of verses fit for those who cannot read,
For those who can do both the field is clear
To meet and trade their wares, the only fear
That mutual benefit might look like greed.

It isn't, though. It's just the interchange
Of showpiece and attention that has been
There since the cave men took pains to arrange
Pictures of deer and bison to be seen
To best advantage in the flickering light.
Our luck is to sell tickets on the night
Only to those who might know what we mean,

And they are drawn to us by love of sound.
In the first instance, it is how we sing
That brings them in. No mystery more profound
Than how a melody soars from a string
Of syllables, and yet this much we know:
Ronsard was right to emphasise it so,
Even in his day. Now, it's everything:

The language falls apart before our eyes,
But what it once was echoes in our ears
As poetry, whose gathered force defies
Even the drift of our declining years.
A single lilting line, a single turn
Of phrase: these always proved, at last we learn,
Life cries for joy though it must end in tears.

Australia Felix

Was it twenty years ago I met that couple
In the Melbourne Botanical Gardens?
In those days you would often see the couples –
Well-dressed and softly spoken, arm in arm –
Of new Australians who had made a life
A long way from the wreckage of their homelands,
But this pair were exceptionally spruce,
Though easily the age that I am now.
They were reserved, but I was curious.
Two Poles, she from an Auschwitz labour camp,
He crippled by the walk home from Siberia,
They met in Krakow, married, and came here
On a migrant ship that docked at Woolloomooloo –
Which must have seemed a long way from Lwow,
Though the old name was in the new name somewhere.
Knowing my face from TV, the man told me
My jokes against the local intellectuals
Concerned about Australia's vassal status
In a Western world controlled by the US
Were falling on deaf ears. "They've no idea,"
He said. She nodded in agreement, graceful
Like my mother, who would certainly have liked her.
"We walk here every day," she said. "So peaceful."
He nodded while he watched the currawongs.
Her first fiancé perished at Katyn,
The year my father sailed to Singapore.

Oval Room, Wallace Collection

Created purely for the court's delight,
Pictures by Boucher and by Fragonard
Still work their charm no matter how we might
Remind ourselves how frivolous they are.

Surprised by Vulcan, Venus doesn't care
A fig, and Mars is merely given pause.
The reason for the cuckold's angry stare
Might be that her sweet cleft is draped with gauze.

Boucher does more of that when, held in thrall
By naked ladies, Cupid doesn't seem
To grasp that he himself could have them all
If he were older. This is just a dream,

Even when Fragonard's girl in the swing
Splays her long legs, kicks off one velvet shoe,
Knowing that boy down there sees everything.
He can't believe such miracles are true,

And here they're really not. In this whole room
All images save one are sex made tame
By prettiness, the pranks of youth in bloom,
Winsomely keen to join a harmless game.

But Boucher's Pompadour is on her own.
Her poise commands us to include her out:
Such swinging scenes are a forbidden zone.
The kind of woman men go mad about,

Even in company her solitude
Was strictly kept. She never spilled a thing,
And what she might have looked like in the nude
No man alive could know except the king.

Always my visits here are made complete
By her, the stately counterpoint to these
Cavorting revellers. Aloof, discreet,
She guards the greatest of the mysteries:

How sensual pleasure feels. It can't be seen,
So all this other stuff was just a way
To take the edge off how much love could mean
To win and lose, back then. Just like today.

Against Gregariousness

Facing the wind, the hovering stormy petrels
Tap-dance on the water.
They pluck the tuna hatchlings
As Pavlova, had she been in a tearing hurry,
Might once have picked up pearls
From a broken necklace.

Yellowfin drive the turbine of sardines
Up near the surface so the diving shearwaters
Can fly down through the bubbles and get at them.
Birds from above and big fish from below
Rip at the pack until it comes apart
Like Poland, with survivors in single figures.

The krill, as singletons almost not there
But *en masse* like a cloud of diamond dust
Against the sunlit flood of their ballroom ceiling,
Are scooped up by the basking shark's dragline
Or sucked in through the whale's drapes of baleen –
A galaxy absorbed into a boudoir.

Make your bones in a shark family if you can.
If not, be tricky to locate for sheer
Translucence, a slick blip that will become –
Beyond the daisycutter beaks and jaws –
A lobster fortified with jutting eaves
Of glazed tile, like the castle at Nagoya
Hoisted around by jacks and cranes, an awkward
Mouthful like a crushed car. That being done,
Crawl backwards down a hole and don't come out.

Numismatics

Merely a planchet waiting to be struck,
The poem shapes up, but is not a coin
Until, by craft, and then again by luck,
He fashions clean devices fit to join
A scrupulous design that he would like
To look mint fresh and not like a soft strike –

It must be hard. "It must be hard," they say.
But no, it isn't, not when you know how.
Except he doesn't. He just knows the way
To scratch and scrape until the coin says "Now",
Boasting its lustrous proof against the sleaze
Of verdigris, that cankerous disease.

The scholar rediscovers the doubloon
Inside the encrustations we call Time.
The critic says it might shine like the moon
But pales in value next to a thin dime.
The poet only knows that he can't cheat
At any point, or else it's counterfeit.

He must be definite yet open to
The second thought. He mustn't make a mark
That falls short of the palpably brand new
Whose play of light pays tribute to the dark –
One solid, spinning, singing little disc
Perhaps not worth much, but still worth the risk.

Nefertiti in the Flak Tower

If there was one thing Egyptian Queens were used to
It was getting walled up inside a million tons
Of solid rock. Nefertiti had a taste of that
Before the painted head by which we know her –
That neck, that pretty hat, those film-star features,
The Louise Brooks of the Upper and Lower Kingdoms –
Emerged to start a tour of the museums
That finished in Berlin, almost for keeps.
It could have been the end, but for the flak tower:
With all the other treasures, she was brought there
And sat the war out barely shivering,
Deep in an armoured store-room built by slaves –
That old scenario again. During a raid
The guns sent up eight thousand shells a minute,
Some of them big enough to turn a whole
B-17 into a falling junk-yard,
But the mass concussion, spread through so much concrete,
Was just a rumbling tremble. In each tower
At least ten thousand quaking people sheltered,
Their papers having proved them Aryan.
When the war stopped, the towers fought one more day
Because the Russians couldn't shoot a hole
To get in. Finally they sent an envoy.
The great Queen was brought out and rode in state
Back to her little plinth and clean glass case.
In Berlin in the spring, I cross the bridge
To the *Museumsinsel* just to see her
And dote on her while she gives me that look,
The look that says: "You've seen one tomb, you've seen
Them all." For five long years the flak towers stood

Fighting the enemy armies in the sky
Whose flying chariots were as the locusts:
An age, but less than no time to Nefertiti,
Who looks as if she never heard a thing.

Spectre of the Rose

Goethe and Ulrike von Levetzow in Marienbad

You see this rose? This rose is not just you,
Crisp in the softness it makes visible,
With all its petals nourished by the dew
That wet its leaves last night and pumped it full
Of crimson lake before the rising sun
Reached down and opened it to be as one
Slow-motion cyclone of sheer loveliness,
Lush yet precise, contained in its excess,
A sumptuous promise to be always new,
Superbly poised as you when you undress:

This rose is also me, condemned to die.
The laws by which its nest of shells will fade
From the circumference inwards, it lives by
And follows to the end. So deep a grade
Of red is bought with borrowed time. The power
Of photosynthesis in plant or flower
That wrecks what has been built works even here,
Captured in such a jewel that it comes near
To matching you. You put it in the shade
I feel advancing with each precious hour.

Below it on the stem, regard the thorns
Meant to protect its frailty while it grew.
Doomed from the moment when the thoughtless dawn's
Fatal initiative brought it to view,
It came here to this vase, and here it glows

For us, and it is yours and mine, this rose,
But it is also you and I. Two lives
United only for a time, it thrives –
Spreading its perfumed beauty as you do –
For just a while, and while it stays it goes:

Perfect too late for me, too soon for you.

The Same River Twice

Surely you see now that you gave your name
To the easy option. Nobody disagrees
About the infinitely shifting texture
Of the world. A malefactor loves the haze
Of boiling chance that blurs the total picture,
The fog you stand in up to your stiff knees,
Looking so wise, as if you'd solved the structure
Of all causality, when you, in fact,
Left out the thing we needed most to know –
That our character will leave us free to act
In contradiction to its steady flow
Only through our regretting that the river,
Though never still, is still the same as ever.
No man steps out of it, not even once.

On A Thin Gold Chain

Opals have storms in them, the legend goes:
They brim with water held in place by force
To stir the dawn, to liquefy the rose,
To make the sky flow. They are cursed, of course:
Great beauty often is. But they are blessed
As well, so long as she herself gives light
Who wears them. Shoulders bare, you were the guest
At the garden table on a summer night
Whose face lent splendour to the candle flame
While that slight trinket echoing your eyes
Swam in its colours. What a long, long game
We've played. Quick now, before somebody dies:
Have you still got that pendant? Can I see?
And have you kept it dark to punish me?

And Then They Dream of Love

"Were you not more than just a pretty face
And perfect figure," he thought, kissing one
While clamped against the other, "this embrace
Would not be so intense." But she was done
For now with doubts and fears. Her state of grace
Had come upon her like the rising sun.
He bathed in daybreak, loving its suddenness,
The way she shook, her look of sheer distress
That meant the opposite, and everything.

Back in the world, her limbs still trembling,
She said it all again, and this time he
Expressed himself in words as best he could –
"You must know you mean more than this to me" –
Merely to find himself misunderstood.
"You mean you don't get lost in ecstasy
The way I do?" she said. "I want to be
All that you need of this." He said, "You said
I only cared what you were like in bed."
And so their bickering began again

About what you mean now and I meant then.
Only so long could they go on that way
Before they parted, worn out by their knack
For petty quarrels even when they lay
Replete. The things they said before came back
To plague them. If it matters what you say
It can't last. Best to take another tack,
And meet for just this, very late at night.
Would she do that? No. He would. She was right.

Beachmaster

Scanning the face of a crestfallen wave
He sees his life collapsing to a close,
A foaming comber racing to its grave.
But after that one, there are all of those:

The ranks of the unbroken, the young men
Completely green, queuing to take their turn
To die so that the sea might live again.
That much it took him all his life to learn.

Propped on her elbow in the burning sand,
The latest Miss Australia views it all
As one vast courtship. With a loving hand
She strokes her thigh as one by one they fall,

Those high walls in the water. Look at her,
But shade your sad glance carefully, old man –
For she will never see you as you were,
A long way out, before the end began.

Continental Silentia

Neat name for the machine
On which the lists were done:
Quietly ordered violence.
Feathers by the ton.

The whisper of a tempest,
The ghost of a parade:
Pan-European silence,
A pop-gun fusillade,

A muted rat-tat-tat,
The excuse already ripe:
We knew nothing of all that.
All we did was type,

And corrections in those days
Had to be done with x's.
You couldn't just erase
And start again: wrong sexes,

Wrong spellings . . . it took ages.
Just to get it right
Meant black spots in the pages:
Blurs of a foggy night.

Unspoken and unsung,
Those names that didn't matter.
Sonderbehandlung.
Just written, pitter-patter.

Continental Silentia
For all those in absentia
Respectable dementia
Sub rosa eloquentia

List, oh list
The rest is silence

Put to silence

Zum schweigen gebracht

Typewriter
Firelighter

Tap tap

Language Lessons

She knew the last words of Eurydice
In every syllable, both short and long.
Correcting his misuse of quantity,
She proved the plangent lilt of Virgil's song
Depended on precision, while his hand,
Light as a mayfly coming in to land,
Caressed her cheek to taste the melody
Of such sweet skin, smooth as a silk sarong.

Give her the palm for speaking well, he thought,
But has she ever melted as she should
With no holds barred, or wept the way she ought?
His scraps of Greek, it seemed, were not much good.
He said the words for rosy-fingered dawn
And when she set him straight with laughing scorn
He spoke a tongue she barely understood,
Contesting her with kisses long and short.

In such a way they traded expertise
Until the day came it took half the night.
She gradually improved his memories
And he set loose her longing for delight.
The passion underneath the verse technique
She saw in its full force, and learned to speak –
Strictly, as always, but in ecstasies.
So finally, for both, the sound was right,

A compound language fashioned out of sighs
And poetry recited line by line.
Few lovers and few scholars realise
The force with which those separate things combine
When classic metres are at last revealed
As reservoirs where rhythms lie concealed
That sprang from heartbeats just like yours and mine,
Pent breath, and what we cry with flashing eyes.

In that regard they made a pretty pair:
He with his otherwise unhurried touch,
She with her prim and finely balanced air,
When they lay down together, came to such
An ending they were like a poem caught
In the last singing phrase of what it sought
To start with: to contain what means too much
Left lying loose. In something like despair,

Though it was joy, they would forget they knew
What anybody else had ever said
Of love, and simply murmur the poor few
Abstract endearments suitable for bed
Until they slept, and dreamed they'd never met
And none of this sheer bliss had happened yet.
One woke the other – which was which? – in dread:
Ah, Orpheus, what has lost us, me and you?

Alas, what is this madness? Out of sight
Like smoke mixed with thin air I seem to fly.
Although her form, when he switched on the light,
Was still there, he had heard her spirit die.
To bring it back, he swore that he would go
To hell for her. It would be always so,
For he would live forever and defy
The halls of Dis and the gigantic night.

Having heard this from him, she smiled again,
And in his arms came back to life as one
Returning to the mortal world of men,
Their ticking clocks, the race that they must run.
Believing in their love: that was the task
That these two faced. It seemed too much to ask,
So moved were they when all was said and done
Knowing that it would stop, but never when.

Peter Porter Dances to Piazzolla

First subject, *The Bank Dick*.
In the New Old Lompoc House
Fields crosses the lobby twice with the inspector.
It means the inspector fell out of the upstairs window.
In a silent film, a title would have said so:
A sound film can say it without words.

There can be word-play even in the desecration
Of an enemy's severed head.
Fulvia shoved a pin through Cicero's tongue.
What she meant was: "Where are your gibes now?"
It would have sounded better than that in Latin,
But the gesture was better still.

Harry Lime's face shifts into the light
Like the Christ of Michelangelo
Floating upward from the tomb.
Resurrection, apparition, revelation
Are among the words not used:
Nor are they by Verrocchio's St Thomas.

Garbo's Camille has drawled "Armand Duval,
Where are my *marrons glacés*?"
While still we're stunned at what she didn't say
When she turned to look at him:
She fluttered, speaking only to the eyes.
Her Queen Christina came from Samothrace.

In the same way that Fields locked off the viewpoint,
The camera stays on the car
While Basil Fawlty goes to get the branch
He will beat it to death with.
No words, not even pictures of a word:
Wittgenstein, move over.

He did, the day he generously conceded,
When faced with Sraffa's Neapolitan gesture,
That its tacit content blew holes in the premise
Of the *Tractatus Logico-Philosophicus*.
A whole position had gone phut
Like the Great Dictator's globe.

Speaking of which, A Bullet in the Ballet
Is a great title, but you have to see it,
Because there is a letter you don't say.
See it, and you've got it to a "t".
Tell you what, let's just quit fooling around
And screw each other instead,

As Antony said to Cleopatra
At their last *bal masqué* in Alexandria.
Were the lyre, the lute, the sistra and kithara
Ever as gorgeous as what we've both just heard?
Sorry I couldn't do that last bit better,
But thank you, it was lovely and so are you.

Silent Sky

Peter Porter b. Brisbane 1929, d. London 2010

The sky is silent. All the planes must keep
Clear of the fine volcanic ash that drifts
Eastward from Iceland like a bad idea.
In your apartment building without lifts,
Not well myself, I find it a bit steep
To climb so many stairs but know I must
If I would see you still alive, still here.
The word is out from those you love and trust –
Time is so short that from your clever pen
No line of verse might ever start again.

Your poems were the condensation trails
Of a bright mind's steady rush of soaring power,
Which still you show. Though plainly you are weak
In body, you can still talk by the hour.
Indeed we talk for two, but my will fails
Before the task of wishing you goodbye.
There's all our usual stuff of which to speak:
Pictures and poems, things that never die,
And then there's history, which in the end
No one survives, not even your best friend.

No one like you to talk about Mozart
Bad-mouthing Haydn: how the older man
Forgave the coming boy. No one like you
To bring it all alive, the mortal span
Of humans who create immortal art:
Your favourite theme. I ought to tell you now

That I will miss you. But I miss my cue,
Unless it's tact, not funk, that tells me how
To look convinced this visit need not be
The last at which you're here to welcome me.

If I am mealy-mouthed, though, you are not.
You say you hate to eat because it feeds
The crab that's killing you. I could well ask,
If only to find out what fear it breeds,
Whether you dread your death now that it's got
A grip the morphine can't shake. That would be
For me, however. Better to wear my mask
Of good cheer and insist Posterity
Cherishes you already while you live,
And there will be more time, and more to give.

Ten weeks? Ten poems? Scarcely, it transpires,
Ten days. The planes can fly again. The phones
That never stopped are saying you are gone.
We try to give thanks that you made old bones,
But still I see the beach at Troy, the fires
For fallen heroes. This is an event
Proving for all the great work that lives on
A great life dies, and leaves an empty tent –
An aching void to measure our time by
As overwhelming as a silent sky.

Special Needs

In the clear light of a cloudy summer morning
A stricken one, holding his father's hand,
Comes by me on the Quay where I sit writing.
His father spots me looking up, and I don't want
To look as if I wished I hadn't, so
Instead of turning straight back to my books
I look around, thus making it a general thing
That I do every so often –
To watch the ferries, to check out the crowd.
The father's eyes try not to say, "Two seconds
Is what you've had of looking at my boy.
Try half a lifetime." Yes, the boy is bad:
So bad he holds one arm up while he walks
As if to ward off further blows from heaven.
His face reflects the pain at work behind it,
But he can't tell us what it is:
He can only moan its secret name.
The Nazis, like the Spartans, would have killed him,
But where are the Spartans and the Nazis now?
And really a sense of duty set in early,
Or at least a sense of how God's ways were strange:
After the death of Alexander
The idiot boy Philip was co-regent
To the throne of a whole empire,
And lasted in the role for quite a while
Before his inevitable murder,
Which he earned because of somebody's ambition,
And not because he couldn't clean his room.
They're gone. I can look down again, two thoughts
Contesting in my head:

"It's so unfair, I don't know what to do"
Is one. The other is the one that hurts:
"Don't be a fool. It's nothing to do with you."
A lady wants a book signed.
I add "Best wishes" –
All I will do today of being kind –
And when I hand it back to her, the sun
Comes out behind her. I hold up one arm.

Pennies for the Shark

Taronga Park Aquarium once had,
When I was very young, a basement pool
Inside a mocked-up sandstone cave. A sad
Collection of big fish would, as a rule,
Just steam around it slowly till the bell
Rang for their feeding time. They didn't eat
Each other, which was strange, but just as well:
They'd had more than their fair share of defeat.

The giant rays, like blankets on patrol,
Deferred to one thing only, the Grey Nurse:
The lone shark, coloured between coke and coal,
Whose very outline spelled death like a hearse,
She was the reason that the pennies lay
So thick on the pool's floor. People would chuck
One down. It slid off, if it hit a ray,
But if it hit the shark it sometimes stuck.

As I recall, the coins in the shark's back
Were flush or even countersunk like screws.
New coins would glint but old ones turning black
Still made their little circle. The real news,
However, was about the ones that hit
The pectoral fins and stayed put: battle scars
In a fighter's wings, or code meant to transmit
Some foreign curse, like messages from Mars,

To pay the shark back for the pain she might
Have caused had she been free to roam at will
And find fish hiding in the reef at night,
Or humans in the surf. Licensed to kill,
She was a draw because she was a threat,
And would have shown you, had you fallen in,
The last thing she was likely to forget
Was how to deal with your white, gleaming skin.

No doubt they cleaned the pool out once a week
And picked bad pennies gently from the beast.
For what she said, she didn't need to speak,
And every year her pulling power increased.
She had to be looked after. You might think
That by the standards of today her life
Was torture, but the way she didn't blink
Told us the *femme fatale* lived by the knife.

Nevertheless I sympathised. Aware
In some vague way that nature suffered through
This notion that an animal could bear
Its prison if the roof was painted blue,
I tossed half-hearted pennies from the rail
Suspecting that she might be sick of things,
That shark, in slow pursuit of her own tail,
Pock-marked with pictures of the British kings.

Butterfly Needles

Having grown old enough to see the trellis buckle
Like an embroidered dress
Beneath so many decades weighed in honeysuckle,
The old man's idleness
Is honoured by this house as he sits late.
Until the fruit bats come he is content to wait.

Here in England, this is a different garden from that other,
Back at the start.
Here you could kick and scream and call out for your mother
Until you broke her heart
And nothing quite the same would come except the butterflies,
And even they with different squadron markings. Expert eyes

Say butterflies at dusk grow dorsal portals for receiving
Needles, or maybe pins.
That sounds to me like Nabokov relieving
The burden of his sins.
Forget about it. Just give me that old nasturtium scent
I breathed when young, and would again, now I am spent.

The nasturtiums, into which my silver Spitfire crashing
Made a banshee noise
But climbed back to my fingertips with wingtips flashing:
None of the other boys
Had anything as good, which made my fighting talk sought-after,
A first taste of the poisoned flower whose cordial is laughter.

Take it easy, mister. Sniff the real estate you're ruling:
You, the last one here.
A butterfly died once and now the whole damned planet's cooling
At the wrong time of the year.
Stand up too quickly and you hear the headsman chuckle
And the words "Sleep well" are far too near the knuckle,
And for your next trick, you will disappear.

Nimrod

Some marched, some sailed, some flew to join the war,
And not a few were brought home on their shields.
My heart is with those voiceless ones. They were
The harvest of the broken-hearted fields,
And I drew fortune from their bitter lack
Of any luck. Silent, my father stands
Before me now, as if he had come back,
While this lament, whose beauty never ends,
Not even with its final grandeur, casts
Its nets of melody to hold me still
Beneath his empty eyes. How long it lasts,
That spell, though it is just a little while.
Then he is gone again. The world returns:
Babylon, where the Tower of Babel burns.

Culture Clash

Beside the uniquely hideous GLC building
On a nasty September day
With a chill in the air and rain just starting to spit,
The Japanese couple, only this minute married,
Have come to be photographed,
The Thames in the background looking as deadly dull
As ditchwater by Dickens. Bill Sykes
Was lucky to get himself hanged
Half a mile downriver from here.
When the sun goes in, it makes falling out of a window
Seem like the thing to do. But just look
At the bride. No, not at the groom, whose suit
Would be a black-tie outfit if not in white
With trimmings a duck-egg blue, the shirt all frills
Like Tommy Steele playing Liberace's houseboy.
I mean look at her. Inside that three-tier cake
Of a dress is a model for Utamaro.
Do they have another ceremony at home
With all the traditional rigour?
And is it a *gaijin* flaunting his arrogance
To wish her lifted out of this concrete mess
And taken home by JAL to the rooms of paper,
The laths of wood and the properly arranged flowers,
With *kimono* and her hair pinned up to frame
The fresh snow of her beauty?
Look at the line of her cheek as once the painter
Would have looked at it in the Floating World
When he spoke to her with the reverence of a duke
To the Lady Murasaki.
Ah, Butterfly, you have failed to understand.
You must not come to us. We must come to you.

Fashion Statement

I see it now, the truth of what we were
Back then when we were young and Sydney shone
Like a classic silver milk-shake canister
Trapping the sunlight in a cyclotron
Of dented brilliance. In our student kit
We were dandies. We just didn't look like it.

This year I almost died. Propped up in bed
I went back to that time and saw them all,
Even the ones who are already dead.
In the cloisters, encamped on the stone wall
Outside the library staircase, we cracked wise
As pretty girls went by, their shining eyes

Lit up, we fancied, by the flash word-play
Of drawling fops who didn't look the part.
But that was what our dress-sense had to say:
Farewell to choking collars. Hail the start
Of dressing down to suit the heat and light.
It took thought, though, You had to get it right.

We wore the first T-shirts. The desert boots,
The lightweight army surplus khaki drills –
These were our standard gear, the business suits
Of young men with no business. How it fills
My mind with longing now, the memory
Of lurking off with endless energy

To read the poets – seldom on the course –
To write a poem – never quite resolved –
To be removed from Manning House by force –
It was where the women were – to be involved
Completely – never fear what might befall –
In the task of doing nothing much at all.

For some, that task became their whole career,
But even they lived better for the style
We forged then over reservoirs of beer
With leave to sit around and talk awhile –
Well, talk forever. So the time slid by
Into a lifetime. Who can wonder why?

And as for those who burned to make a mark,
We made it with the tongue we mastered where
It felt like daylight even after dark,
So soothing was the heat, so sweet the air:
The perfect atmosphere for epigrams
To flaunt their filigree like toast-rack trams.

To see the harbour glittering in the sun
Like fields of diamonds and the squall arrive
Across the water sudden as a gun
Was bound to bring the optic nerve alive
Searching for words, and we who wrote them down
Might not have looked it, but we owned the town.

For nothing rules like easy eloquence
Tied to the facts yet taking off at will
Into the heady realms of common sense
Condensed and energised by verbal skill:
It has no need to check before a glass
The swerve of a frock coat around its arse.

Already ugly and with worse to come
Yet lovely in its setting past belief,
The city got into our speech. Though some
Were burdened by their gift and came to grief,
And some found fortune, but as restless men,
We were dandies. We just didn't see it then.

Paper Flower Maiden

Screwed up in every sense, she occupied
The smallest space that she could organise:
The country mouse of all church mice. Inside,
Her soul, whose only outlet was her eyes,
Was dying of compression sickness. Then
She met him, the most confident of men.

Her agonies of manifold self-doubt
Were foreign to him utterly. One touch
From him, and she began to open out
Like a chrysanthemum. This is too much,
She told herself: I'll use up all the air.
He kissed her mouth and she was everywhere,

A tide of petals that filled up the hall
And climbed the stairs. She screamed to be put back
The way she was. He, trapped against a wall,
Struggled for breath till everything went black.
He woke to find her gone. The trail of scent
She left behind her everywhere she went

Led him towards her but he never quite
Caught up with her, until he realised
She was the flower garden which, at night,
He roamed in, half entranced, half traumatised
By how the beauty he'd set loose had no
Need of him now, yet would not let him go.

On Reading Hakluyt at High Altitude

High in the stratosphere, I speed toward
Australia's share of history's cruelty,
Reading of caravels with priests aboard
Who landed on Ormuz to hack a tree
Into the deadly stakes that served the sword
Of Christ the Merciful, his soldiery,
And captured Christians died, though, truth to tell,
Our Great Queen likewise would have marked for hell

All sailors who were not True Protestants
Had they been less intent to spread her name
World wide, in script light-footed as a dance
To us, but back in those days smoke and flame
Wreathed every letter. Be it high romance
Or merest greed, unless they're both the same,
That drove the ships of old, they crashed and burned
Or fed the fishes when they overturned.

The Portuguese, the Spaniards and the Dutch,
And all the times the English almost made
A landfall on our land-mass – it's too much
Drowning to think about, a sad parade
That leaves you with a throat too dry to clutch,
Sensing the flesh dissolved, and bone decayed –
But really we should shift our starting date
To further in the past. It's far too late

The way it is, and serves the fond idea
The cloudland of our gentle indigenes
Was wrecked when we decided to come here
To exercise our new-found ways and means:
Just name the day and Lo! We would appear
Out of the surf like Hollywood marines
Sprinting ashore in roughly half the time
It takes to find a rhyme or plan a crime.

But it took centuries for men to find
The means of even failing on the waves;
It took the murderous patterns in the mind
That made a mockery of Jesus Saves;
Above all it took industry, the kind
That limes the sea lanes with a million graves.
The quick did not usurp the slow, the quick
Had just grown slightly slower to get sick.

Visit the flight deck? Asked, I always do
Not just because the toy trains never die
As thrill-providers, but because it's true
That how we sailed is still there when we fly,
In the controls. All that Magellan knew
Is in those panels, carried eight miles high
By turbo-fans whose climb to power began
With just the wind, and just the mind of man.

How unimaginable the past seems.
When read about in detail! All that pain
With little gained or even less, the schemes
To get rich quick turned rotten by the rain –
Or ruined by the lack of it. All dreams:
Except the few that worked gave us this plane
We fly in now, our voyage just begun –
To catch the giant sling swung by the sun.

The Buzz

Grown old, you long still for what young love does.
It gives the world a liquid light injection,
A sun bath even in the night. The buzz
Blurs brain-cells by infecting everything
With lust. A girl bright as an egret's wing
Will cleave unto an oaf and see perfection,
And as for him, don't ask. He thinks her thighs
Open on heaven and his hands have eyes.

Time will sort all that out, but what a loss!
Sweet reason is our name for sour reflection,
The pause for thought that kills the fairy floss.
With luck, there will be two of you to trade
Tales of the star-burst that could never fade,
But did, and give a voice to introspection:
Which is love too, though not quite the young kind
We comfort ourselves now by calling blind.

But there is nothing young love fails to see
Except the future. Bodies and their connection
Are all creation, shorn of history.
These are the only humans who exist.
Whoever thought to kiss or to be kissed
Or hit the sack from every known direction
Except them? Visions radiantly true
Don't change with age. Those that have had them do.

Dreams Before Sleeping

The idea is to set the mind adrift
And sleep comes. Mozart, exquisitely dressed,
Walks carefully to work between soft piles
Of fresh horse-dung. Nice work. Why was my gift –
It's sixty years now and I'm still obsessed –
Hidden behind the tree? I cried for miles.
No one could find it. Find the tiger's face.
It's in the tree: i.e. the strangest place.

But gifts were presents then. In fact, for short,
We called them pressies, which was just as long,
But sounded better. Mallarmé thought "night"
A stronger word than *nuit*. Nice word. The fort
Defied the tide but faded like a song
When the wave's edge embraced it at last light.
Which song? Time, time, it is the strangest thing.
The Waves. The Sea, the Sea. Awake and Sing.

Wrong emphasis, for music leads to sex.
Your young man must be stroking you awake
Somewhere about now, in another time.
Strange thing. Range Rover. Ducks de Luxe. *Lex rex.*
The cherry blossoms fall into the lake.
The carp cruise undisturbed. Lemon and lime
And bitters is a drink for drinkers. Just.
I who was iron burn in silence. Rust.

What would you do to please me, were you here?
The *tarte Tatin* is melting the ice cream.
One sip would murder sleep, but so does this.
Left to itself, the raft floats nowhere near

Oblivion, or even a real dream.
Strange word, nice question. Real? Real as a kiss,
Which never lasts, but proves we didn't waste
The time we spent in longing for its taste.

Seek sleep and lose it. Fight it and it comes.
I knew that, but it's too late now. The bird
Sings with its wings. The turtle storms ashore.
Pigs fly. Would that translate to talking drums?
Nice if they didn't understand a word
Each other said, but drowned in metaphor –
As we do when we search within, and find
Mere traces of the peace we had in mind.

Forget about it. Just get up and write.
But when you try to catch that cavalcade,
Too much coherence muscles in. Nice thought.
Let's hear it, heartbreak. Happiness writes white.
Be grateful for the bed of nails you made
And now must lie in, trading, as you ought,
Sleep for the pictures that will leave you keen
To draft a memo about what they mean.

You will grow weary doing so. Your eyes
Are fighting to stay open. When they fail
You barely make it back to where you lay.
What do you see? Little to memorise.
A lawn shines green again through melting hail.
Deep in its tree, a tiger turns away.
Nice try, but it was doomed, that strange request
To gaze into the furnace and find rest.

Incident in the Gandhi Bookshop Café,
Avenida Corrientes

They were all dying for her,
But they died bravely, they died well.
It was well done.
I was proud to join them.
We all went over the waterfall together.
We fell together.
The world fell together.
For a sacred moment it was all one,
And then she was gone.

Briefly she had sat there
Making notes to mark her progress
Through the labyrinths of Borges –
Something in her manner
Discouraged offers of help –
And then she looked at her watch.
Did she have a lover somewhere
Or perhaps a tango class?
Imagine being the maestro
Against whom she leans
In a tensile *puente*.

Deep breasted, long legged,
Silk skinned,
She was the kind of beauty
Who makes every poet
Wish he were a painter,
So as to say:
"Take off your clothes:
I need the essence of you."

Old poets who try that
Get themselves arrested,
Whereas painters never fail,
Until the day they drop,
To score with the girl of fine family
And the perfect behind.

Having paid her bill,
She stood up and was swept away
On a wave of sighs
As we all shared the light in our eyes,
Our hearts bleeding,
Before going back to the books
We were writing and reading –
Back to the usual macho shit
Which is all there is
When you get down to it,

Out of the cloud
Into which the angel
Disappears,
Having blessed us once
With the holy presence
Of her good looks:

Eternity compressed
Into one sweet minute.
She was out of this world
And we are in it.

Now we must begin again.
Poor us. Poor men.
The waterfall:
It was our tears.

The Falcon Growing Old

The falcon wears its erudition lightly
As it angles down towards its master's glove.
Student of thermals written by the desert,
It scarcely moves a muscle as it rides
A silent avalanche back to the wrist
Where it will stand in wait like a hooded hostage.

A lifetime's learning renders youthful effort
Less necessary, which is fortunate.
The chase and first-strike kill it once could wing
Have grown beyond it, so some morning soon
This bird will have its neck wrung without warning
And one of its progeny will take its place.

Thinking these things, the ageing writer makes
Sketches for poems, notes for paragraphs.
Bound for the darkness, does he see himself
Balanced and forceful like the poised assassin
Whose mere trajectory attracts all eyes
Except the victim's? Habit can die hard,

But still the chance remains he simply likes it,
Catching the shifting air the way a falcon
Spreads on a secret wave, the outpaced earth
Left looking powerless. This sentence here,
Weighed down by literal meaning as it is,
Might only need that loose clause to take off,

Air-launched from a position in the sky
For a long glide with just its wing-tip feathers
Correcting for the wobble in the lisp
Of sliding nothingness, the whispering road
That leads you to a dead-heat with your shadow
At the orange-blossom trellis in the oasis.

Vertical Envelopment

Taking the piss out of my catheter,
The near-full plastic bag bulks on my calf
As I drag my I.V. tower through Addenbrooke's
Like an Airborne soldier heading for D-Day
Down the longest corridor in England.
Each man his own mule. Look at all this stuff.
Pipes, tubes, air bottles. Some of us have wheels.
Humping our gear, we're bare-arsed warriors
Dressed to strike fear into the enemy,
But someone fires a flare. Mission aborted.
On the airfield, the chattering Dakotas
Have fallen silent. Jump postponed again.
Stay as you are. Keep your equipment on.
When cloud and wind are OK in the drop zone
We hit the sky and leap into the dark.
Meanwhile just hunker down and get some sleep.
Look on the bright side. Everyone's still here.
The longest corridor is full of us,
Men of the Airborne going back to bed
For just one more drawn-out *Walpurgisnacht*.
Our urinary tracts hung up to drain
Throw amber highlights on the bare white wall
Until another dawn. The sky looks clear.
Dakotas cough when they start up, repeat
Themselves like women gossiping. But wait,
Where are the women? What do they go through?
They fly there by Lysander and get caught
Like Violette Szabo. Out there on their own.
Best not to think of it, stick with the guys
And shoot the bull about your CLL

Leukaemia that might hold off for years,
The hacking rattle of COPD
Which sounds as if it might star Dennis Franz
As Andy Sipowicz, but it turns out
To be the bug they once called emphysema.
The way I smoked, thank Christ it wasn't cancer:
I caught one break at least. It's dawn again.
The sky looks clear. The kit bag full of piss
Is heavy on your leg. Your name-tags itch,
The cannula inside your elbow dangles,
The patches for electrodes decorate
Your chest like Nicorettes. When you go down
Into the dark you'll see it sliced with flak
Just as the bumping Cat Scan bangs and crackles,
As the MRI inscribes the night with fire.
My outfit one by one in the green light,
Out of the door and down into the dark
They go, and not much later in the year
I'm watching Peter jump. The flak comes up
And pulls him in. But no green light for me.
I'm home in the Dakota and the same
Long corridor leads back to bed. More stuff
To hump: omeprazole and doxycycline
Pills for my lungs. The medics give me leave
To be there for my daughter's New York show.
I step ashore and wake up in Mount Sinai,
Felled by the blood clot I brought off the boat.
For ten full days and nights I lie and watch
The Gulf spill oil on CNN, which is
An oil-spill anyway, and back in England
I add syringes to my weaponry.
Bruises from Clexane like Kandinsky abstracts
Blotch me with blue and yellow and bright pink,

A waistline from the Lenbach Haus in Munich.
The women of my family watch the clock
To make sure I shoot up at the right time:
All in the timing and a simple plan.
Normandy showed, and Arnhem showed again,
The Airborne tactic was a death-trap. Crete
Fell to the German sky troops but their losses
Were too great and they never jumped again.
At Cassino and in the Hürtgen Forest
The *Fallschirmjäger* were brought in by truck.
Up in the air like white blooms on a pond
We're asking for it. Borneo was waiting
For the Aussies to jump into if the Yanks
Held back the bomb. The jump postponed,
You see them now in the long corridor,
My countrymen, their incipient melanomas
Cut out and sewn up, scars like bullet holes.
You want to see mine? In the final hours
At Dien Bien Phu fresh paratroops went in
Through tracer veils as if about to land
Slap in the middle of SS *Das Reich*.
They're here again. They must have been patched up:
Not one less handsome than Alain Delon
In *Purple Noon*, but barely half his age.
The Hitch is with them and I hear him speak
Exactly as he looked the day we met:
The automatic flak came bubbling up
Like champers, dear boy. Overrated stuff.
I watch him standing there in the green light.
It switches off. Has he come home with us?
I can't see. I just see the corridor
And my white room. Another night alive
To lie awake and rue the blasphemy

By which I take their deaths as mine, the young
Soldiers of long ago, in the first years
Of my full span, who went down through the dark
With no lives to look back on. Their poor mothers.
Where are the women? Nurse, my bag is broken.
Sorry, it's everywhere. She mops, I cough,
She brings the nebulizer and I sit
Exhaling fog. Dakotas starting up
Make whirlpools in the ground mist. Too much luck,
Just to have lived so long when I unfold
And shuffle forward to go out and down
The steep, dark, helter-skelter laundry chute
Into that swamp of blinking crocodiles
Men call Shit Creek. Come, let us kiss and part.

Book Review

Dante Alighieri: Monarchia
Edited by Prue Shaw for the Società Dantesca Italiana, 2009

More valuable than all of mine, your book
Is neatly kept like everything you do:
So clearly worth the twenty years it took,
It sparkles. Fonts well chosen, margins true,
Its every creamy page exhales the sense
Of learned judgment, tact and permanence.

If Dante waited seven centuries
To see his Latin tract receive such care
He can't complain, though being hard to please
No doubt he did while he was lying there
Still exiled in Ravenna, still annoyed
That so much effort has to be employed

In re-establishing what he first wrote.
But what could he expect? He worked by hand,
And other hands, on skins of sheep and goat,
Made copies, and those went to every land
In Europe, and were copied once again,
And soon for every error there were ten.

Tracing the manuscripts back to the first
Few spin-offs is as good as you can get.
Often you don't get that, and at the worst
A copy's copy's copy's the best bet,
And so the scholar must compare, contrast,
And from the past deduce a deeper past.

It takes far more than sweat. It takes a mind
That can connect with the great poet's heart,
Knowing his sweet new style was spare, refined,
Tough, difficult, precise in every part,
And therefore apt to be fudged in its gist
By scribes half qualified and some half pissed.

Such minds are rare, and often in disguise
They come into the world. My only role
In your brave saga is that I was wise
Enough to see the brilliant scholar's soul
Shine through her beauty in the lecture hall
Even before we met. I guessed it all.

How could that be? Well, here is how it can:
You took notes at the same speed that I ate,
With an eye for truth unknown to mortal man,
Especially this man. It was my fate
To fish the surface but my luck to see
You hungered for a deeper clarity.

I saw you flower in Florence. That was where
The bigwigs spotted you and marked your card.
The sage Contini knew you were a rare
Natural philologist worth his regard,
And while you learned, you taught me. From the way
You read me Dante I foretold today.

Today, so far from our first years, I bless
My judgment, which in any other case
Is something we both know I don't possess,
But one thing I did know. I knew my place.
I knew yours was the true gift that would bring
Our house the honours that mean everything:

The honour of our daughters raised to treat
All people with your scrupulous respect,
The honour of your laughter and the sweet
Self-abnegation of an intellect
That never vaunts itself though well it might,
And this above all, lovely in my sight –

Pursued through busy days in precious hours,
Pored over word by word and line by line
Year after year with concentrated powers
Of selfless duty to the grand design
Of someone long dead who was well aware
That dreams of peace on earth must court despair –

The honour of the necessary task
Done well, not just for show, and done for keeps.
Could I have helped you more? Don't even ask.
I can hear Dante, grunting as he sleeps:
"You are the weakling and you always were.
If you would sing for glory, sing of her."

Whitman and the Moth

Van Wyck Brooks tells us Whitman in old age
Sat by a pond in nothing but his hat,
Crowding his final notebooks page by page
With names of trees, birds, bugs and things like that.

The war could never break him, though he'd seen
Horrors in hospitals to chill the soul.
But now, preserved, the Union had turned mean:
Evangelising greed was in control.

Good reason to despair, yet grief was purged
By tracing how creation reigned supreme.
A pupa cracked, a butterfly emerged:
America, still unfolding from its dream.

Sometimes he rose and waded in the pond,
Soothing his aching feet in the sweet mud.
A moth he knew, of which he had grown fond,
Perched on his hand as if to draw his blood.

But they were joined by what each couldn't do,
The meeting point where great art comes to pass –
Whitman, who danced and sang but never flew,
The moth, which had not written *Leaves of Grass*,

Composed a picture of the interchange
Between the mind and all that it transcends
Yet must stay near. No, there was nothing strange
In how he put his hand out to make friends

With such a fragile creature, soft as dust.
Feeling the pond cool as the light grew dim,
He blessed new life, though it had only just
Arrived in time to see the end of him.

The Later Yeats

Where he sought symbols, we, for him, must seek
A metaphor, lest mere praise should fall short
Of how the poems of his last years set
Our standards for the speech that brings the real
To integrated order dearly bought,
Catching the way complexity would speak
If it had one voice. This, he makes us feel,
Is where all deeper meanings are well met,
Contained in a majestic vessel made
Out of the sea it sails on, yet so strong
We never, watching it our whole lives long,
Doubt its solidity. All else may fade,
But this stands out as if it had been sent
To prove it can have no equivalent.

Even his first things were wind-driven boats.
A coracle would have its speed enhanced
By some queen elf who stood with gauze shift spread,
Materialising from the twilight mist.
Slim dhows, as his romantic urge advanced,
Sliced through the East. A little navy floats
In his early pages. Sleek sloops joined the list
When more substantial things asked to be said.
His wild-swan racing schooners heeled and ran
Cargo from Athens, Bethlehem and Rome,
Or the body of an Irish airman home
Across the gale. The full soul of a man
Was on display: sound craft of trim outline
Criss-crossed the billows. All of his design,

These would have been enough to make him great:
The caravels that reached Byzantium
Alone proved him unmatched. Then, at the heart
Of this flotilla, as if light were haze,
Something appeared to strike the viewer dumb:
A huge three-decker fighting ship of state.
Acres of air caught in her tiered arrays
Of raw silk, she made clear, in every part,
All of her million parts were cleanly wrought
To fit together with no need of nails.
From gun-decks upward to top-gallant sails
She was one artefact, a cloud drawn taut
By force, so far beyond its builder's mind
It felt for him, and saw where he was blind.

Tea-clipper-tall but at the waterline
Three times the width, she had the looks to quell
Resistance instantly by show of might:
Empires would knuckle under. Ireland
Itself would kneel to see her breast the swell
With such bulk. But develop and refine
This image as we may, and as we planned –
Down to the shining brass, sheets chalky white,
Glazed lanterns, mullioned windows, oaken rails –
It will not serve the turn without a sense
Of brute strength tempered by benevolence.
The monarch reigns supreme because her sails,
From cinquecento chapel walls low down
On up through salon panels to her crown

Of screens, woodcuts and painted fans, are all
Unchallenged masterpieces. Her curved hull
Was moulded by the cave walls of Lascaux
And stamped with its motifs. But what we hear,
Not what we see, confirms the miracle
And makes the metaphor. We're held in thrall
By music. Music lush, music austere,
All music ever heart-felt, holds the flow
Of splendour in one place. Not thought alone –
Thought least of all, because it was his fate
To grow more infantile as it grew late –
Could build this thing, nor was it cut and sewn
Or hewn solely by touch, or sealed by skill.
A feat of the self-sacrificing will,

The peaceful man of war is here to prove
Any attempt to emulate her air
Of grandeur invites ridicule, unless
We, too, pour everything into the task
Of building something that will still be there
When we are gone. And that means all we love
And more, as Yeats knew when he wore a mask
To quell the self, thinking its pettiness
Could be faced down. It can't, but it can be
Tapped and diverted to an empty space
Where something permanent can take its place,
Shaped for the voyage to eternity
Out of our tears of weakness at the way
The thing we mean means more than we can say.

Worse than absurd, then – witless, in the end –
To trace him through his visionary schemes
And systems, or pay grave attention to
Those last affairs, boosted by monkey glands,
His patient wife scorned as a dotard's dreams
If more unreal. No scholarship can mend
The error of not seeing all demands
For human truth are vain. Few things are true
About the life except the work. Yeats found
His final glory when his jade and gold
Were joined by rag and bones to sink and fold
Into the flux of images and sound
That formed a magic ship to win the war
Against time, which is just a metaphor

For the battle to make sense of growing old,
And bless the ebb tide. It is outward bound,
Fit for the launch of what we have to give
The future, though that be a paltry thing.
Our house is flooded and our books are drowned,
The embers of our passion are stone cold,
We count the minutes we have left to live,
Yet even now it is of love we sing,
And for a paragon we have the vast
Swan-songs of Yeats that brought his depths to light.
Among school children or on All Souls' Night,
Humble or proud, he saved the best for last
And gave it to the waves – but no. There is
No ship. Just words, and all of them are his.

Habitués

Some older people like the ship so much
They pay again and go wherever it goes –
Which means that for a large part of the year
They just steam back and forth across the Atlantic –
Until they die, while other older people
Are there for one performance after another
Of *The Sound of Music*. They know every word.
"How" they smile wryly as they sing along,
"Do you solve a problem like Maria?" If
They conk out before the interval, are they
Removed? Surely the mark of the habitués
Is that they're dead already. When I noticed
That my club was full of men who had become
Stuffed armchairs and oak tables for school food
I resigned to save my skin. They liked the place
Too much. They thought the ship's Entertainment
Officer was entertaining. They were dewy-eyed
Instead of loud with scorn when Liesl's suitor
Expressed in terms of chaste and tender love
His youthful urge to get into her pants.
Dull death, the minimum of information –
Where entropy, to steal a phrase from S. J.
Perelman, fills every nook of Granny –
Will come when it will come, but while we're waiting
Beware the lapse into familiar comfort,
All outlines softened. In that cloud lies proof
Your life was lost on you, though I suppose
It isn't only easier but better
To echo an ecstatic singing nun –
Transfigured like Bernini's St Teresa

At the mere prospect of an edelweiss –
Than to puzzle out the dialogue of, say,
Act I, Scene IV of *Cymbeline*, which no one
Has remotely, since the day that it was written,
Enjoyed or even partly understood.
And are there no more thrills? In the fjord
The wrinklies crowd the rail to hear their voices
Come back from walls of ice. Couples hold hands.
So quick to guess their last heat is long gone,
How sure are we the failing is not ours,
Our cold contempt a portent of the void
Which is the closed heart and begins within us?
It doesn't always take time to go nowhere.

Castle in the Air

We never built our grand house on the edge
Of the Pacific, close to where we first
Drew breath, but high up in the cliffs, a ledge
Glassed in, with balconies where we would be
Enthralled to watch it hit the rocks and burst –
The ocean that still flows through you and me
Like blood, though many years have passed since we
Sailed separately away to keep our pledge

Of seeing what the world was like. Since then
We've been together and done pretty well:
You by your scholarship, I by my pen,
Both earned a living and our two careers
Paid for a house and garden we could sell
For just enough to spend our final years
Out there where the last landscape disappears
Eastward above the waves, and once again

We would be home. We've talked about that view
So often we can watch the seagulls fly
Below us by the thousand. There's the clue
Perhaps, to what we might do for the best:
Merely imagine it. The place to die
Is where you find your feet and come to rest.
Here, all we built is by our lost youth blessed.
This is your gift to me, and mine to you:

Front windows on a trimly English park,
A back yard we can bask in, but not burn
As we loll in our liner chairs. The bark
Stays on the trees, no wood-pile is a lair

For funnelwebs. Small prospect of return
Once you're accustomed to the change of air,
The calm of being here instead of there –
The slow but steady way that it grows dark.

Sleep late then, while I do my meds and dress
For the creaking mile that keeps my legs alive.
In hospital I'd lie there and obsess
About the beauty of this house, and still
I love it. But I feel the waves arrive
Like earthquakes as I walk, and not until
I'm gone for good will I forget the thrill –
Nor will the urge to start again grow less

As always in my dreams I spread my chart
In the great room of the grand house on the cliffs
And plot my course. Once more I will depart
Alone, to none beholden, full of fight
To quell the decapods and hippogryphs,
Take maidens here and there as is my right,
And voyage even to eternal night
As the hero does, made strong by his cold heart.

Iliad!

*(from a fragment of an ancient manuscript recently
discovered in the ruins of Los Angeles)*

Then well-toned Brad of the head wider in the jowls than in the
brow, Brad of the digitally enhanced thigh, addressed his army of
computer generated warriors, saying: "Computer generated
warriors, merely because the city we besiege is suddenly full of
water would you fall back? Are you afraid of Kevin?"

With these words he put heart into his army, but on the
battlements of the city now full of water Kevin of the small-
chinned tallness called up the goddess Angelina of the exaggerated
curvature and the extensive self-harm, asking: "Are you with Brad
or with us?"

And Angelina of the improbably luscious lips said: "First you
must fight the battle, and then fate will reveal who is to be
preferred."

And Kevin's lieutenant, Dennis of the maniacal laughter and
armless jerkin, said: "What kind of deal is that?"

But already the arrows and the cross-bow bolts were raking the
battlements as with a harrow, and at the gate the way was open for
the chariot of Mel of the hair extensions and the deficient anger-
management to enter, bouncing over the heaped bodies of the
defenders.

So doing, Mel of the augmented coiffure and the inappropriate language, resplendent beyond all others in his kilt and chain-mail tank-top, cried out his war-cry in one or more of the many dialects of which he was a master: "Och aye, wetback trash. Will ye nae face my wrath?"

And his chariot, a Volkswagen under-tray with a Chrysler hemidome V8 engine, bucked and snorted, even as the Kawasaki jet-ski bucked and snorted between the knees of Dennis of the demented cackle. And stricken by the glittering shafts flung by Mel of the irresponsible invective, Dennis of the psychopathic hilarity went over backwards into the water and his life fled.

Now from the tent where he had long been brooding came Keanu of the impeded sinuses. And Keanu of the approximate diction, instead of saying, "Dere's a bob on duh bus," as he had been wont to say, this time said: "Dere's wadder in my ten."

And then to his side, soothing his forehead with elegant fingertips, came light-stepping Saffron of the massive appeal to women as well as men, telling him that the fate of the city depended on his valour.

Having considered this with the plucked channel between his eyebrows furrowed by the pain of thought, Keanu of the inexact elocution replied: "Dere's wadder in my ten." And Saffron of the slim wrists admired by women as well as men knew grief. But even as he spoke, Keanu of the long black leather coat and the blurred enunciation had risen into the air.

Turning upside down, Keanu of the repetitive aerobatics made his way through the whirling swords of the warriors of Brad of the inverted skull, he who had trained them all in the fighting techniques employed in the act of love by himself and the goddess Angelina of the well-concealed tattoos.

Cooperatively shouting to announce their presence and hostile intent, the warriors were kicked in the face one after the other by Keanu of the retarded speech and infinite martial arts skills until so many of them lay floating that they formed a pathway for Kevin of the tattered postman's uniform and Saffron of the soft mouth desired by women as well as men to make their way to the citadel.

For on the steps of the citadel, leaning into the divinely inspired wind which blew only in the close shots so as to outline her bosom in its casing of chiffon and cunningly wrought wire, stood well-stacked, fabulously bottomed Angelina in her gold cloak and ill-advised gold platform boots as worn when taking the form of the mother of Grendel of the ice-bound northern lands.

"Our cause is doomed," sighed Saffron of the doe eyes adored by women as well as men, and Angelina of the unfeasible pulchritude said, "Stick with me, yielding and fragrant one," as her inconceivably curvaceous rack palpitated, almost as if Kevin of the long thighs and the shyly retiring lower jaw were not there.

Then Naomi of the dark elegance and the irrational anger let fly her telephone at Russell of the neck wider than his head and the equally irrational anger. And her telephone was encrusted with sharp precious stones but his telephone was heavier, so both were struck grievously in the eyebrow and their lives fled.

And the Terminators fought the Predators and the Predators fought the Aliens and the Aliens fought the Transformers and the Transformers fought the X-Men and the X-Men fought the Orcs and nobody cared. And Natalie of Naboo had a new hairstyle even more hideous than the last but nobody cared about that either because her quest for new dialogue had failed.

And so it was that on a thin rope, from one of Ilium's topless towers to another, swung Tom of the bared teeth and the built-up boots, but the boots were too heavy by far and when he landed he slid off the edge of the tower and began to fall. And Viggo of the pronounced masculinity said: "Somebody should do something." And Orlando of the less pronounced masculinity said: "Yes, they should."

But then the invaders faltered and drew back as the giant silver air chariot of well-preserved Harrison of the hat, whip and determined maxillary musculature emerged from the billows, drawn by three hundred thousand horses. Astride the silver air chariot's vast and glistening back, Harrison of the even more fiercely focused eyebrows than in any previous scene cracked his whip and called for silence.

And there was silence, even from Mel of the loose mouth.
Spreading as a lack of noise spreads in the leaves of trees when the
storm dies, there was a deepening stillness from all except Dennis
of the hysterical mirth. Restored to life by a breath from Poseidon,
Dennis of the psychopathic merriment rose from the water on the
dripping wreck of his jet-ski, and cried: "Don't let Gary Oldman
on the plane!"

So the water retreated, and there, lying in the mud, ready to be
gathered up and burned, were the corpses of all the poets who had
ever been under contract to write epics. A vulture tasted one of
them and turned away.

A Spray of Jasmine

Political developments in South East Asia, 2010

The day of her release, Suu Kyi wound flowers
Into the hair behind her head: a spray
Of jasmine. She looked lovely doing so,
Something a man my age can safely say,
For she is no child. Who knows if her powers
Extend to the real world? We have to go
On what we see, the people's thirst for her.
Today no junta general would look good
With floral attributes, or hear his name
Made music by the crowds, and if it were,
The reason would be drearily the same
As always, and too readily understood:
The crowds would be afraid. Her graceful calm
Means gentleness, as long as we recall
That Comrade Duch, who also has his poise
And clean-cut looks, for all he lacks her charm,
To most of us meant nothing much at all
When separating children from their toys
In his quiet way. Brought to the killing tree
And smashed to death, they saw a face to trust.
As cool as ever, all humility,
He now denies his guilt. Because we must –
Led by the hand of history as we are
Into the prison where the innocent
Die of their agony so very far
From all our thoughts, no matter how well meant –
We give our hearts to her for being there.
Such beauty has to be benevolent:
Look at her face, the flowers in her hair.

Madagascar Full-Tilt Boogie

The lemur that bit a piece out of my daughter
When she was a student here
By now is dead and gone,
But the island still has lemurs of every size.
A lemur not much bigger than a cicada
Swallows the cicada
As you just might park a Humvee in your hallway.
The cicada gets tons of time, on its way down,
To think "Sod this for a game of soldiers."
Larger lemurs, aloft in the spiny forest,
After feet-first triple-jumps through the parched air,
Land on a booby-trapped branch without their pads
Being even slightly punctured.
It must be done by quick adjustments,
Unless the spines go in and out and leave
No wounds. But then where would be the point,
If that's the phrase we want, of so many needles
Even being there? It would be as if, at Anzio,
Schu-mines had popped up only to serve coffee.
In this dried mud nothing pops up at all
Until it rains, and hey! It's mating day.
A million brown frogs magically appear.
Then half the brown frogs suddenly turn yellow
To indicate their wholesale macho readiness
For a no-holds-barred mass fucking.
Brown females politely yawn while their admirers,
Having dished out Nature's usual idea of passion
In less time than it takes to blow your nose,
Go back to being brown
Like the population of Rio after Mardi Gras.

You can't leave out the dressing-up factor.
The chameleon, proceeding along a branch
Like the second act of *The Family Reunion*,
Reminds us of the bad year T. S. Eliot
Wore green powder on his face
When greeting guests for dinner.
The whole damned island is choc-a-bloc with shape-changers.
Have you noticed that sick parrot over there
Is wearing John Galliano's face before last?
We should cut the poor bastard some slack.
Hitler, after all, started out as a dress designer
And never went near anti-Semitism
Until the critical failure
Of his first couture collection . . .
Don't look now, but in the third fork from the top
Of the tree behind you is a lemur
Doing a fair imitation of Coco Chanel.
A bit too cute perhaps,
Like Audrey Tautou in the same role.
She's coming down. She wants someone to pat her.

Bubbler

A lifetime onward, I know now the bubbler
In the school playground said things in my ear
As I soaked up the coolness with pursed lips.
"Bellerophon, framed by rejected Antea,
Has slain the Chimaera."

I was too young to know these whispering
Refreshments were the classic voice of time
Drenching the world. But it got into me
Somehow, and when I wiped my mouth and chin
My lips were tingling with the urge to speak.

The bubblers, a generation later
Fed girls of Asian origin with the rush
Of ancient love-talk as they stood tiptoe,
Their cheeks awash. "The coolness of the night:
It penetrates my screen of sheer brushed silk
And chills my pillow, making cold the jade."

Remember the brass guard to stop your kiss
Short of the dribbling bulb?
Yes, and I remember Aphrodite
Fresh from the bath, as the maths star Pam Yao Ming –
Who married an insurance man in Cabramatta –
Remembers the Shang Dynasty.

A Bracelet for Geoffrey Hill

A standard day's haul from the burial mound:
Quartz cat's eye cuff-links for a chain-mail shirt,
A Stalin button and an Iron Cross.
Small treasures liberated from their dirt.

Elsewhere in Mercia, a king prepared
For death took off his belt and doe-skin shoes,
Unzipped his lap-top, cleared security
And in the lounge sat back to watch the news

Until his flight was called. The galaxies
That showed up in the Hubble Deep Field frame
On long exposure shine like pick'n'mix
Sweets in their coloured shapes, no two the same.

Thus thrives the densely wrought. The cloth departs
And leaves the cinch more complex on its own:
An all-star inscape spinning precious wheels
In lattices of bronze, gold, pearl and bone.

Subrius Falvus, Tribune, last to die
When the plot to topple Nero came to naught,
Knelt by the grave that had been dug for him
And saw it was too shallow and too short.

Ne hoc quidem ex disciplina. So
He speaks in Tacitus. "No discipline
Even in this." When stripping a Bren gun
Brush clean the butt-plate for the firing pin.

Coherent multiplicity takes force
For which the reader must be made to care
By how it sounds, or else it's just white noise.
The symphony that lovely women wear

Next to the skin gains weight when taken off
And folded flat with tissues in between.
From tight arrangements we deduce the role
That each part plays, if not what it must mean.

We only know that here the heat contained
Speaks volumes about what was seen and felt
And still astonishes, more now than then –
Before the buckle came loose from the belt.

The word-lord, fresh in from America,
Lectures in Oxford. He knows everything.
Note-taking Helen shivers at the thought
She'll be outlived by her engagement ring.

The Shadow Knows

See how the shadow of my former self
Moves through the kitchen, putting plates away.
The dishwasher yields up its treasure trove
Of future shards from long-ago today.
The blue-ringed soup bowls go home to their shelf.

I get home often now, as shadows are
Inclined to do, because they are so weak.
Now that my work is done, the peace I love
Is here for me, and you can hear me speak
More clearly now than I spoke from afar.

I am the shadow and the widower
Because the innocent you were I slew,
But you are here, and real, and far above
My level of attainment. It is you
Who brings me back to love what we once were.

Grief Has Its Time

"Grief has its time," said Johnson, well aware
It was himself he spoke for. Others must
Be granted full rights to a long despair
Fuelled by the ruination of their trust

In a fair world. A child born deadly sick
Or vanished: psychic wounds that never heal
Ensure that wit, though it once more be quick,
Will not be merry. Pain too deep, too real.

Free of such burdens, I pursue my course
Supposing myself blessed with the light touch,
A blithesome ease my principal resource.
Sometimes on stage I even say as much,

Or did, till one night in the signing queue
An ancient lady touched my wrist and said
I'd made her smile the way he used to do
When hearts were won by how a young man read

Aloud, and decent girls were led astray
By sweet speech. "Can you put his name with mine?
Before the war, before he went away,
We used to read together." Last in line

She had all my attention, so I wrote
The name she gave me, which I won't write here,
And wondered how I'd come to strike the note
She'd clearly heard in poems that were mere

Performances beside the hurt she'd known:
Things written for my peace and my delight.
"Be certain, sir, we take a deeper tone
Than we believe. Enough now for tonight."

Out in the street he spurned my proffered arm:
His cobbled features caught the link-boy's flame.
"The love of God can get no lasting harm
From fear of death. The two things are the same."

Yet all the way home he pursued the point
As if the argument about God's will
Within him made him ache in every joint
Until he reached the truth and could be still.

Utmost concision, even in a rage;
Guarding the helpless from experiment;
Stalwart against the follies of the age;
The depth of subtlety made eloquent –

These were the qualities of Johnson's mind
Even the King felt bound to venerate,
Who entered through the library wall to find
The rumpled, mumbling sage, alone and great.

Vision of Jean Arthur and the Distant Mountains

Look back and you can almost pick the minute
When the last power and spring of youth withdrew,
And you began to walk, not run,
Searching ahead for places to sit down.
Really it's been the one long day since then,
But gradually invaded by this peace
By which you are looked after. The light ebbs
As it does before the heavens open,
And the air fills with this strange comfort,
As if there were a soft and loving voice
Putting sweet emphasis on just one word
To mark the moment of your growing old.
Shane,
You can't just stand there in the *rain*.
You'll catch your death of cold.

The Light As It Grows Dark

The light as it grows dark holds all the verve
That you were ever thrilled or dazzled by,
But holds it folded thick, stacked in reserve.
More for your memory than for your eye
It brings back pictures that your every nerve
Once revelled in while scarcely caring why.

You care now. Time has come, and there will be
No light at all soon, so look hard at this:
Behold the concentrated panoply
Just here in this small garden's emphasis
On colour drained of visibility.
In daylight, such wealth might be what you miss.

The flowers are growing dark, but they will live,
And so will you, at least a little while.
Good reason you should do your best to give
All your attention now. It's not your style,
I'm well aware, to be contemplative:
The thought of chasing shadows makes you smile.

And yet I swear to you each figment had
Full meaning once. The images are here
That made your day when you would run half-mad
For too much good luck. Now they reappear
So fragmentarily you find it sad.
But really it's all there, so have no fear:

The light as it grows dark has come for you
To comfort you. It is the sweet embrace
Of what your history was bound to do:
Close in, and in due time to take your place.
You can't believe it, but it's nothing new:
Your life has turned to look you in the face.

Plate Tectonics

In the Great Rift, the wildebeest wheel and run,
Spooked by a pride of lions which would kill,
In any thousand of them, only one
Or two were they to walk or just stand still.
They can't see that, nor can we see the tide
Of land go slowly out on either side,
As Africa and Asia come apart
Inexorably like a broken heart.

We measure everything by our brief lives
And pity most a life cut shorter yet.
Granddaughters get smacked if they play with knives,
Or should be, to make sure they don't forget.
So think the old folk, by their years made wise,
Believing what they've seen before their eyes,
And knowing what time is, and where it goes.
Deep on the ocean floor, the lava flows.